To B

GW00854089

UNCONTROLL
F

with
love

Steve .

For Lala, like the last one

UNCONTROLLABLE FIELDS

Steve Griffiths

SEREN BOOKS

SEREN BOOKS is the book imprint of
Poetry Wales Press Ltd
Andmar House, Tondu Road
Bridgend, Mid Glamorgan

*The publisher acknowledges the financial support of
the Welsh Arts Council*

Typeset in 11 point Palatino by Megaron, Cardiff
Printed by John Penry Press, Swansea

CONTENTS

Acknowledgements

are due to the editors of The *Anglo-Welsh Review, Radical Wales, Poetry Wales, Stand, 2 Plus 2, New Welsh Review, Picture: Welsh Poets* and *The Poetry Book Society Anthology, 1990.*

RIVERS ARE RUNNING BENEATH US

Cars line up over the buried Fleet,
agents of dubious liberty

riding on air,
tethered with gravity.

Below, a mole
noses the femur

of a long-murdered
Constable of Moorgate,

cudgelled in former
meadowgrass then

in one fluid move,
purse and throat slit.

Silvered, the grasses
bent their heads under the moon.

The wife never knew.
She haunts briefly:

the matter was not so deep.
Nothing hears

the mole's small cry
among the foundations.

MUSEUM PIECES

1. Bath Museum

This large-limbed symmetry
would once have been vested
with the healing trimmings of power,
as the gold grain oozed
from the sumptuous live pores
of merchants lounging at poolside,
doing business with religion and refinement.
On a high wind, swimming pool laughter
and horseplay burn my ears.
As the news from Rome faltered to static,
they put their gold against decay:
a process akin to dentistry,
precision engineering
in the uncontrollable fields:
now an amusement
and an inaudible calling,
persistent as the gentle
grating of archeologists
among mechanical diggers.

Craft souvenirs, the Goddess of Wisdom,
the curative salts and the pedigree fish.
A crowd shuffles respectfully
under spotlights
on walkways
between broken stones,
redolent of aftershave and anorak,
served with mosaics and deities
out of the rain.

A moment to absorb them:
the Gorgon and Minerva flash by
like Tube destinations
bereft of their roar:
clockwork shocks on the Ghost Train,
daylight robbery
as the doors bang sudden as life and death
behind you.

We grub among relics with the certainty
of a pig rooting,
for illumination in a metaphor
with a museum afterglow.

The stones resonate softly
with the subdued passage of herdsmen.
Visitors are drawn to the river,
deer come down to drink.

Here's one, squatted naked among the reclining
fragmented limbs of the giants' work
taking his shit with confident disregard
surrounded with his animals
and the nuzzling, acrid steam of their dung
become dew.

I leave my offering with the other
subterranean smells,
the animal traces,
the sweat under nylon,
the soil under nails.

2. Museum

The infants' class grow
among boarded sweatshops
and the nests of charred beams
that make hearths out of houses,
among ruined yards
harried by quarrels and radios.
The pigeons are silent and corrupt,
diseased adaptors.

3. Chernobyl

The passing of time is increasingly cavalier,
it sounds like the shunting of trucks.
My friends deserve better
but I fear for us with decreasing patience
locked in a museum
in tumbling rockfields passable
only on foot,
drowning faces pressed on the vapoured window.
There are few merciful delusions
in their last mouthed 'o'
and their scattered possessions,
rooted where the rock burns through.

4. Shadows of Potency

Customers queued for the museum
like a line of pincered things
crawled out of the sea

to view a relic of pearl
phalanges in a frame of earth
half buried, clutching a Nikon,
a familiar returning our monstrous
flashcube glances that still the past,
define, comfort, confirm,
mirror the stuck flash of the sun.

Here are the blacks running and shouting
past armoured cars in Soweto.
The stiff whites eye them
from their potent tomb.

On scored walls painted bison
reflect a bounding primary hunger
through a receding window:
stagskull on manskull, itinerant
families dance an event
to wound an image for sympathy:
fingers weave and crowd the air, point
and bring down the running beast
its altered hide scoured and sung
small, innocent of a past.

By the round white grubs of the missile farm,
from the exoskeleton bunker of the ant,
photograph the stuck flash of the sun,
take the memory wherever you make your home.

GLYNDŴR SUBDUED

Burned out, there was no road back,
and the flames of Sycharth brought Glyndŵr
dreams enough:
his home was a country now,
the revenges multiplied.
The helicopter's shadow,
a great hare
runs fleetingly across a field –
the grass panicking, flattened,
trying to disperse but unable.

Almost an experiment,
the disciplined ructions of the first raid,
the strained respect for brawny lives
a delicate line: Rhuthun settlers,

robbed and dishevelled, emerged
to a heady, bright, small Welsh triumph
reeking of sheepshit
and soot in the bright sun:

insults counted, it was a homely,
small, scared, village altercation
as shoving and grunting skirmishes
around slag once made history.

The victors clattered away
shod heavily with expensive curses
to where even the sparks on the hill
were drunk down by the mud and the dark.

Later the conscripts, cast-off and dangerous,
sported their rusted dream of omnipotence,
hacking for their neglected fields
and their friends cut down,

and then for the riven cold in their bones
women ran in the wet grass
brought down like deer with cries of triumph.
People ran blindly,

made his, the pervasive guerilla
reeking of smoke and prophecy,
the peaceloving fire
displaced in his rafters.

The banging of shields,
plastic and leather,
rang in his ears:

war war war sle sle sle
went the childish wailing of sirens
in the gusting wood,

and the night's drunken instruments
scoured the wet streets
for the Welsh doggis and their whelps.

An English city listens behind curtains
to the running and breathing, the slugging
thud of quarry cornered and floored:

the resistance is
that we will not turn the television up
in tribute to the night.

Divided loyalties, undermined
meal-tickets, sprouted on hillsides,
the weeds Indignation
twined with deep-rooted Ambivalence

picked for the same dish.
Drenched resisters sidled in droves
along valleys to give themselves up
to the straggling columns of troops and grain.

When the fighting is over, the land of dreams
is a table lit with unshareable faces,
a once-in-a-lifetime
remembered meal to the hungry:

a looted peacock under the arm
of some big, sharp-featured
father of mine
who dried his eyes at the flame of Sycharth.

Then the withdrawal to memory
of the fair people, walled in the clouds
of exile within, the retreat to mystery
of the fair times on their vague upland tracks.

Glyndŵr had to master this potent
trick of retirement, to the light
in a dolmen glimpsed rarely and late,
a light in the mind

where sometimes he lingers noisily in the grid of years
and the speed and charisma growl in him
to the applause of the shingle in the undertow,
old chimera whose wait has a tide's hypnotic

push still. It breaks
in like the sudden clatter of leaves
of a kneeling army

or a belief in the mountains upturned,
with mirrors,
lit from inside with our own light.

The poem uses the chant of the northern English students at
Oxford, heard by Adam of Usk, at the beginning of the Glyndŵr
uprising:
          "War war war, sle sle sle
            the Welsh doggis and their whelps".

VILLA-FAMÈS, AUGUST 1986

for Fernando Almela and
i.m. Alberto Solsona, 1943–88

Red, soft-rock strata cut a line
of niches, shelters, age-creases
and navels in dry, strewn terraces
of erosion and collapse.
In hardened powdery space
abandoned to hawks and foxes
we were easily scattered
among fossils.
Our voices indiscreetly
defied the undersea silence
among the winds, and were lost.

In a decorated overhang
a chipped half-circle of stick-men
move with serious staves and appetite
through layers of memory and smoke.
It's their blood inundates the streets
from flood-channels high in the town.
With an arrow through him
a bull rears and falls forward
in ochre and blood,
surrounded in the grey bushes.

The afternoon gone badly awry,
firecrackers, beercans and oildrums
crash through the last of the bull's mind.

Neatfooted, barrel-chested, tossing
star on a rope with a minder, he came in
to the faces leaning forward to applaud
and the leafing back of old men
in their irony and knowing pride
for boys their children raised
who stretch and thrust and crow
their hips seasoned with wine and panic.

Their fast trainers touch
the edge of the bull's reach
to provoke the girls with fingers sucked
between their teeth:

the bull keeps coming,
he's a boxer with the odds stacked
and the crowd applaud its dreams,
his breathing
sorely intimate and provoked.

He bursts up the stairs, over a barrier
scattering runners into back yards
breaking sanctuary.
Women wave red towels for him
and he looks for his escape in lizard cracks.

He's down again, quick and light
and goaded by the curious flapping of a hat:
he fills a gap between spars
with his jarring distended trophy of a face.
He leaves a last mark in the wall of a cafe'.

Only his tail and flanks move
and a scribble of flies
that ride his heat.
There's a questioning
unsteady stillness.

Through a field that blossoms handkerchieves
and hands to catch his eye, he turns
to begin his last passes
to the small men running away
down his long vista.

The halter's ready.
Behind him are stick-men who poke and shout.
A beercan clatters towards him.
A father holds up his little girls to the bull.

He's wound in closer on a line
towards the butcher's laundered shorts.

The murdered bull goes up to the square,
becomes hung meat on a cross,
is elected mayor and presides
over a music shrill, lopsided, steely
with a movement of hips for his death.
There is subtle food in the clarinet and saxophone,
there are stately dark shades
on dining chairs, dressed for a nativity.
A slow colouring from the throat
of a trumpet hovers round

intimate parts that glisten in buckets
and probably reflect the stars above,
however faintly.

Six fiesta queens relax
beyond the arc lights, lounging
doe-eyed in their self-belief;
six official virgins off-duty,
marriageable somewhere between tonight
and the eighteenth century,
decorated with good hope,
strapping daughters in shawls
of intricate lace,
the village fixed on them
with carnival tenacity
to invest in and honour their vigour
of weathered figureheads
with green shoots and a lick of paint,
their grandmothers' gold combs in their hair.

Through flaking teeth of rock
that lay broken on hillsides
run imprints of movement,
rushes of stone, stills.

A lean fox turns to watch
women once honoured
bury the thin resilience
of their voices in ploughed land ·

Dry clouds crackle their long storm

like a leaf in the fist
over a parched line of almonds.

A video trained on coils of blue plumbing
in a bucket by the fountain
summoned the gut-stirring curiosities
of the Civil War:
those farmworkers who carried out
centuries of the bodies of saints and nuns
and arranged them
interestingly, in daylight
in the plenitude of their inheritance.

Scavenging in the early chill of the square
the fox looks up to the silent windows
and the sleepers behind their eyelids of stone
where blood dries quicker than music.

ELEGY FOR JOHN TRIPP

A man on the radio talked of soft tissue
printed on million-year riverbed
like a morning-after mattress –
and I thought of you very clear, John,
lifting a pint of dark in some dolmen basement
regarding the sudden answers of the morning
after your stealing away, your sharp face
set in that spirit of mock astonishment
you learned to bewilder
producers of talks and tired assumptions.

I remember a belated urgency
in your face, as it turned back
watching the cultivation of soft edges,
as history, its fares paid, took off like that taxi
we tried to hail with a borrowed carafe.
There was a march full of friends' banners
and irony, probably sodden,
with a brass band and a cock-up somewhere.

On a stand in another world
the unprofitable take an unremitting review
of their leaders.
You take the salute, spilling drinks
and blood and atonement, and you break the silence
with what nearly everyone felt,
snarling at flummery, throned, waxing manic
then tender as warm buns in a paper bag
with some small forgiven fault
from your recognised gallery.

Confusion and moral astonishment,
something unfinished, an obvious instruction
unlearned: you listened and stirred tea
to the huge roaring ironies
of shopping bag conversation
as the rust-red deep shit rose at the window.

Then you slotted the poems accurately
in the darkness between laughing teeth
in darkened smokefilled rooms
like some young boy who, they said, had
"immaculate positional play";
like the occasional sun through the steamy
windows of your café,
illuminating the brown sauce and the salt.

And you planted your ground of demands
that you never sold
for one moment of narrow-angled comfort,
brambles round tanks.
Your green armies
knitted their sharp-eyed peace,
needling hard minds,
weaving, digging, planting,
still they work and plot:
they move down out of the hills' cover
laughing their experienced laugh.

MAJOR POWERS AT HEYFORD

They vaunt their hammer-drill mastery
across pristine bird-morse, these fighters
on the edge of the continental shelf,
and the mowers' smoothing wash of lawn
and the silent grooms with their horses' sharp steps
pause in respect, watching
trapped birds in the world's house
fly at a mirror.

In Steeple Aston
dumb with its own lush self-esteem
I'm taken back
by a kindly organic thatcher
to the ridge of a garage roof,
clutching my little certainties
like tenuous lichen
as a Vulcan bomber drifts down
slowly enough to think time's stopped,
unicorn-white,
moth-nocturnal with dusted wings,
that fragile.
H-bombs had something special in them
the shape of rugby-posts,
and I knew these Vulcans had them aboard.
I'd heard gunshot from woods
but I knew from the air it was cleaner,
that distance picked things white like the sea,
and cleaner's what we stood for.

Over the fields I ran after the Comet,
the Vampire, the Gloster Javelin
with its camouflage, the lofty things
with hawk-noses, the masked pilot
and helmeted conqueror, Cabbage White,
Tortoiseshell, Red Admiral,
and I collected the cards from packets of tea.

And now it has come to these boys, decked out
in their armour delicate as flies,
bearing their savage captions
from my comic book
that curled brown on the kitchen range-
it's all in there:
the man who blessed the congregation of planes,
the quiet sufficiency of cockpit data,
the editorial decision:
Gadafy's adopted daughter whited out
with the corrosive innocence of distance.

CONTINUITY

I dreamed a tiger
in a suburban tennis court
pursued me with ominous grace
and quiet hunger.

The wraith of my son's hand
raised at my shoulder:
he had been eaten whole
but kept coming, a whiteruffed silence.

I ran, breathless
with that curious infant sense
of disembodiment:
I was the dead boy at my father's shoulder

gathering sinew in the corner of his eye
like firewood as it turned colder,
too keen
to be merely confined or devoured.

THE HUNTER'S APOLOGY

Antler-branch, oak-bulk,
the monster is guided down the stairs
at the birthday party
to scatter the children's small arms
with his misfiring thrill of fear.
He nearly topples, and groans
under a muffling tower of eiderdown.

Somebody else's daughter grips me
her little fingers bind like a reed,
momentary daughter,
river never crossed.

The game is to steal
the jewels from under him
as he crouches and waits, blind
with his stick:
it's all beyond you,
the lord of the hunted
with his pack
that mill invisibly in the garden.

Now with a neighbour's comforting, slow embrace
the tall antlerman leans forward
to say sorry:
you'll have none of it,
he will not lie down all night,
the trapper, handing out beads,
you will take none for your mother.

All night Snow White walking the paragraph of her death
like a corridor full of the masks of butterflies,
the last page torn out, doorway to morning,
then the wingbeats of suburban geese pump and echo
carrying a pack of souls for the far North.

Upstairs in the quiet
a child is drawing a monster
he dreamed he was frightened
to become.

FATHERS

Animate and silent, columns of rain
wheel slowly off the mountain.

My friend sits twitching like poultry,
male tears hoarded, unlocked now
their late gold burns
then streams down to his five year
pull between warmth inherited
that had to be worked for, inhabiting history
like children asleep
after taking the day at a run,
and the roughshod and ridden, uncertain
power of gay self-discovery:
those boys' arses moving before him
buds and mirages grown substantial,
the familiar form in the dark bed
finally unreal.

Unable to touch his family,
the confused, unpardonable loving recoil
cauterised with guilt's daily charge.
He found no reliable words for the dark
encroaching, and the light bothered him:
the echo of trees on an empty lake
harried him back to the cliffs of mother.

On the day my father left us,
his barrel-chest brooked no question:
he directed the photographs and the trains
and the angle of the sun.

But although I was there,
I was too difficult to be snapped at four.
Later, held up on a bridge, the driven smoke
of another shining monster blasted my eyes.

When I was ten my mother told me
he must have died, and that was true
till the close old deity put forth shoots again:
those hidden years he'd compressed a massive chord,
his round weight on the black-and-white keys
of the Bechstein he owed a student for,
a continuous layered humming inside me
till, all power and slowfired resurrection,
relic and animal,
he pawed at the lid and the brandy:
I was flung back twenty-five years
to the hesitation of four.

My friend drove with me to the shuttered village
of my grandfather and his unmentioned brothers.
Nothing happened
but a white horse by a stream,
a farm on a ridge
and a church without a roof.
The hawthorns pointed and waved
their freckled white
like airport spectators
at the harsh blue bearing down
till we covered our eyes.
An awkward visit, a warning.

We drove back through abandoned workings,
through an archeology
softened with explanation.
Throat full with his tearhoard,
in a dream my father tells me
it could have been so different,
his mute hands smearing the childhood ivory.

UNMETALLED ROAD

In memory of my father, 1893–1984, composer.

He went when I was four:
there were a few stamps from Africa
that bore the reassuring orange tree,
the one I believed money grew on.

Responses are grafted and trained
but they take their own curious flight:
ashes clouding the wind,
they become a shared thing,
a spilled thing.
Like cattle in churned mud,
the wreaths breathe on each other
in a corner of intimate sustenance,
lowing their silent farewell.

The past darkens and advances like a wall,
lightfooted creatures moving behind it.
Old and stooped, he knew the score
and it's buried and his,
music lingering like gas
or a secret body under an old floor.
His city reverberates in taut wood
and burns, it is long gone Belfast,
he takes it with him in a mason's box.

He creeps past my narrow bed
in the dark, looking at me with rare
tenderness among barks of prejudice,
a goblin with the rotating eye of a lighthouse,
a mastery of empty searoads.
The wall holds its breath.

He bobs by on the night
and I try to make of him
something less than a monster, small but imposing
appeared suddenly from far out at sea.
Damp-eyed reminiscence floats in, regrets
and boasts each hiding the truth like a room
viewed through glasses of brandy.

Old foghorn on full sail
he goes by grandly preoccupied
with his voices spread along Gothic ceilings
outward like palm leaves in cathedral spaces.

He leaves me with his unvisitable
crag of complaints and psalms
which stand in their own time:

making allowances for age and a thoughtless
and ruthless desire for only the best
I listen for the quiet haunting of his blood.

A BETTER PLACE

Between the wars that engineered
his generation and cut him
uncomforted away
from the docile house
he might have tethered his mind to

he and his bike pushed decently
at the obliging hills. He slept outside
lashed in a starry wind then
ambushed by renewing needles of rain
while the view retreated towards him
up the dim, wholesome valley.

Now I heard him piss at the bathroom wall
with his back to the ghostbowl
and the wallpaper swelled
and darkened its pattern in evidence.

He frowned at his piece of cheddar:
"This is very bad fowl".

Talking the past through
in a wintry jungle of frequencies
the words impaled the yellow snow
thawing off him
with their shabby incontinent barbs,
markers of age on ages,
a ghost nun walking through hedges.

"There are too many slaves,
we'll have to get rid of a few" —

was it interference,
did some hard-eyed captain
his apple-face dried to essentials
by skin trade moaning in long holds
call at our living-room,
come for him?

Big decisive men who happened
to be passing, like cromlechs,
dragged him out with a gentleness
born of custom,
and he shouted his betrayal
to the walls of the house
clearly for the last time,
sending his birds wheeling
for the last time:
"Not fit, none of you".

Under a cloud they drove away
with a wasted man counting suddenly
lucid grievances under blue sheets.

We had let him leave his glasses:
when he had them on
he was trying to walk through walls
through a landscape lit with chaos
shot through with dutiful bruises,
diminishing wishes,
hardhearted silence.

I came in through traitor's gate
to a relief
that keeps coming to meet me
with his eyes across the narrow yard.

HOME FIRES

Creeping toward night
your Florence Nightingale candle
casts a flowering angle
on your rakish plastic bath-hat,
unshadowing your stubborn eyes
in a young girl's face,
always, we said, your advantage;
the certain path straightened out
and down behind you
like a downturned mouth,
petering out on a cliff
where you appeared to me
under the oblivious flocks,
surrounded by believed-in books.

The motor of your life,
the lid on your life
was to be able to say
you had done your all
for me and my brothers.
Children who could not let you down
guided and justified:
the irrefutable heroism
urging upward toward the light
like the steam from your hands
in a sinkful of dishes.
Where have we gone now, children
with the damage or debt forgotten
in our frightened pockets,
the unreachable urbanity,
the inverted adulthood wherever we look

from our dungheap indulgently down
towards our impudent children
or to the grandparents marooned on the dry hill.
Your protective, working absences
I filled with the wordless intricacy
of small crabs in a sheltered pool,
advance and retreat, pincers raised,
aggressive and curious on fine sand
among outcrops of hanging wrack
that extended like tugged-out knots
of hair on the furtive swell.

When you were five
your mother came to see you
after a year away
teaching an elementary grace
among the grown-up crash of the bombs.
You rehearsed your equilibrium
with drawing-room remarks,
drilled by a bombasine aunt.
Two paces forward,
your hand outstretched:
"Good afternoon, mother;
and how is father?"
Buildings unsupported
on the train home,
you fell on each other.

You were never able to say what you wanted,
you kept up your guard for the uncertain
ghost stalking your happiness,

you planted and sharpened your own
stakes and husbands
to limit and protect what you could do.
You refused to refuse
to refuse.
My father knew nothing of this,
heatseeking crusader
with his gift of your vulnerable trust
and your passion in the thrust of his confidence
under his arm in an overnight bag:
entitled to nothing
you accepted a promise gallantly meant
and desertion, trained for resilience
with no-one there to confirm or recognise
anything in you but motherhood,
and that thrown at you
as my father's guests walked past
thinking you were nothing
because you were on your knees, cleaning.

Your hip-bone china,
the clenched white joints of your fingers
never gave as the work built up
an unrealisable store
in the beyond, a stone
smoothed and chipped alternately
by passing hands.
You typed and cooked
with a brittle vigour,
with a reticent hope scrubbed
into surfaces where lodgers passed

in the hall's obscurity,
carrying their own bags:
customs man, shoemaker,
teacher, small town theatricals
who trailed a guttering phosphorescence
in the shadows of their former lives
below the searching white-light of the vestibule,
their futures out before them,
motes and fishes under divers' lamps:
sometimes they crossed yours.
Their parties raised a roof with a gleam,
the meadhall of your clamouring, buried palace
confronting the flattened dunes
and the sea's worrying monologue
in the early half-light,
set against effortless ballads
on strung-out toilet-rolls,
lost and envied.
Dawn rose
with your freckled strong arm
and a yellow duster.

After the man of blood
strode menacingly through
the hours of darkness on my stairs,
Snow-White's real mother's ball-gown
breathed and rustled a bird-headed comfort,
here was the work and the dream of my mother,
the power sewn by tired fingers
at the end of the day,
the low point gathering for triumph

in the penultimate phase,
its echo pressed without end now
in an evocative pile
of dog-eared historical romance.

The dream moth-pattered against glass
till it found an opening:
you resounded with urgency
to the caked makeup, the macs
with turned-up collars and the smokers' coughs
of the village hall,
to your own ear,
small and warm and a credulous pink.
I partook, breathing the perfume
of a star in the frost,
of cushions and cold leather
late at night in the taxi home beside you,
beside the annunciation
of the suspended sea.
And I didn't like it
when you played an old woman,
and they powdered your hair grey
and floured and wrinkled your face.
I didn't like it any more than you do
where you sit
a little apart from your family
unsure of whether to be proud
upset by the cameo grandchildren
with huge voices
at the furthest end of a made prospect,
folding away the vigour of your past
like summer clothes.

Your head inclines to the downbeat,
the blind white larvae burrow
through dark grained rings,
sealed by the boatman
set out by the sandman with the sack
trudging low-water horizon
for bait, set adrift
in the seamless nightthroat of the sea,
curlew and dogbark chiming out
their irregular spirit-time.
Sometimes I was your voice in the dark,
seeking warmth
as I padded in and you took me
sleepily to your bosom,
me and my scuffed trunkful of toys,
my unending desire
for the people who put the dew there.

You carry your age in a brimming cup
sustained by no more than a surface tension,
a hesitant severity,
a faltering reach towards us
turning back on itself
your weak eyes fixed on
the curling page of the horizon.

Nodding, you sink back
letting your arms
and your hair stretch out in the water,
girlhood voices piping and pattering
in your wainscot veins.

Page by page,
armour reclining by armour,
I see you with my father in your death,
in my child's joinery, all thumbs:
facing across river,
across pillow, across binding,
the harbour lights reflecting
cats' fire,
the truth in the bondweight,
the complex meshing of the waves,
their smoothing out
a puzzling emptiness.

THE GUESTHOUSE

In a living hold
of legs and table-spars
I hugged my knees and listened
beneath the long table-talk
to the creaking of seasoned joints,
the friction of thighs in nylons,
to my mother's nerve
carrying the spirit of the house
through the stir and grate of coffee-spoons,
the guests diving for wit's minnows,
the spirit of the house carrying her nerve.

The past is swallowed, or crystallised
like laughter caught in the bottom of a cup,
to be washed out or examined
till the particles dance:
the trick pyjama-man hung from a light
who faced the sea in a darkened room,
the laughter that ran down
a sweating kitchen wall
like a thrown egg
or caught the skin like sea-holly
planted between sheets.

After the meal,
we ran with the dogs on the sand,
we knew nothing, suspended,
their pink tongues lolling at speed
past the washed-away gravehill.
Under the sea were the overrun stumps
of a forest, at low water
you could see the swimming heads

of bladderwrack
and this was how the forest of Welsh
drifted away perversely
on an incoming tide,
receding as the rafts crossed Menai,
a waterbird beyond the trees
striking distance and terror
in the invading troops
for this densely populated language
of fogs and yellow grass.
My dogs ran towards it,
barking to enter
through the long sealight,
from the bleached coastways
into the hard bark
and the leaves that drip
their stickiness into open mouths,
but there was nothing where they stood:
oystercatchers quivered their limit
in the tide-edge light.

We blushed with sweat,
spiky-haired and sand-encrusted
in the shop at the end of the beach;
we were tormented across the sweetjars
by some unattainable thing of
lace and fulsome violets,
her chaste Welsh poise
so very clean, our shyness intact
as tender breasts encased
in the firm imaginary government
that she exercised over us,

and we ran back to a vigorous system
of dams and canals
that we built and destroyed repeatedly
from a rivulet that leaked out under a rock
and spread across the sand to meet the tide.
We made a prosperous broad swathe
of yellow crops and minerals
with buried trees and relics,
full of small hidden scenes:

here, a boy looked up at the locomotive
his father, refusing to be lifted up
to the footplate for the dirty
brilliance of the anthracite that burned
with integrity from every face,
and it rode away, taking its power
to be smashed in the waves;
here a boy waved a stick amazed
as the tall cattle sauntered like liners
under his power in deep mud
(here a group at the piano echoed
the suspended bite of good harmony
into gathered corners)

and we yelled as level after level
of our world collapsed
beneath the waves that crashed and curled
over the clouded faces of the lakes –
you could see people running
on the listed decks of a steamer –

we yelled and rebuilt,
the sea at our elbow
sated mischievously
with ships pulled over in the night,
a great sow that smiled and fawned
in the adulterous shallows
that lapped the sand from under her nipples
at dawn, small waves purling over her.

Now, my creations lie about me
in a guest house room,
found and set out
as ornaments of porcelain and brass:
selected acts and losses,
the deceptions
that passed over your head
in a living ship of adults
with the dry pollen of cheek and groin
there among pods dropped
round a vase on a sideboard.
It could be a place of silent attrition
as downstairs the ghosts take tea.

On the cropped, wine-dark lines of the carpet
I push my Maserati to its limit:
how the tyres hold their bends,
the commentary's roared out
to a distant knot of voices
woven with radio choirs
on some bar of time, where rows
of mothers are calling us in late
from the dunes,

where the shell of a church
is sturdily beached,
little humblecake walled round
above the tidal rocks by a testing site,
pointing west out to the migrations.
In the shrunken timber of the door
high-coloured boys in uniform
have gouged and left their mark
beside the grated stones of the bay.
Small yearly services,
the rare flap of a cassock
hold on to a residual power in the air
by what remains of the causeway
there among the disordered shingle.
Turned on the sea,
the land's curved bowl reverberates
after the passage of a fighter.
I add my name and leave
pursuing dishevelled saints
in cauldrons of wind.

TRYING TO LEAVE BODMIN

I circle around Bodmin
thinking how places become mine,
watching it from above:
the streets crawl up towards me
in a stony mist
that fingers and rolls up towards the moor,
all of it cupping my mother in her last days
as her reach upward diminishes.
I find brothers on the roads above the town
and the road out
but they will not leave;
they do not know each other:
you must be up there early
to catch the silence of it.
After the third stroke she said
that her body was too long
to exercise her feet.
That's why the brothers can't reach
all the way down to where she lies.

A FLOURISH LIVED

There is a good death,
we have it in us.
The pictures around her
were joined by some of their subjects,
peering over the lip of the bedspread
far above. She reflected their faces
back to them, though sometimes
she hadn't the strength:
I clattered a few words past her,
stones into water, horses through a wall,
it didn't matter, she slipped away.
The wind is sweeping and blowing the spray
off the crests of the rollers,
back out to sea. My mother's arm
was a long and giving bridge
with the veins and skin hung from it,
in evidence. There was just
the signal of a thumb,
moulding our hands faintly
over an intimate distance.
It sought to milk the hills for comfort.
The undertow of her pulse
dug and sucked and arched back
down into the next groove and rib of sand
and the next, with the huge fluttering
of the ocean dragged back into itself
spread out inside her and silting towards
a hard black knot in the creamy foam.
There were eyes to call on
for absolution, but she would glance,
in passing, into the room

from the street, through lace curtains
and not see us. Then the memory
of a chemical fog closed in,
the trains of chlorine through Amlwch
and their slow clatter, our faces
lowered over vapours of hot tea.

The last look was mad and wild,
it was a two-way piercing black
as fresh as the dew, an impersonal horror.
The midwives at the gates
paused in their cleaning of her,
they said it was right, it was luck,
don't forget to say goodbye,
the last recognition that we and she
would carry forever.
They told me to hurry and kiss her.
They were triumphant. I cut loose
and they went on with her for hours
into another country.

The hymns had been old sofas,
tolerated with embarrassment.
This was another grief:
they began to trail stuffing
when she needed the sustenance
of conviction. But she was away
gathering at the brambly edge
when she took the blessing of the young priest,
his cassock long and black, the beard red,
and there was no way of telling her sigh

but they said it was comfort.
The hymns made a good blaze
at the funeral, she could hear us in there,
first a jolt then our noses lifted
past the strain of our throats,
the fields through the clear glass blurred,
she would have enjoyed that.

The coffin at last is at home with itself,
the pine, its handles perhaps of brass
and its burden.
It goes off alone
on the unpretending absurdity of rollers
into a sunset of curtains,
our hands no longer holding,
nor the shouted hymns.
Brought home by mechanical toys
the inexplicable truths are animate,
and the lessons crush in like mourners
in a small space, craning upwards
for a future that never arrives on time.

She loved the flourish
of our harmonies over the washing-up.

Our farewell is encapsulated
in her last, shaking welcome
arranged there in her best,
in a powerful recess.

VIEWS FROM THE CHAIR

1

The assistant daisy-trips around the chair,
she wears her reassurance
frivolous and large.
The gun-dog eyes of the dentist follow her
through long drill-silences
over impotent mouths and half-closed eyes.
Her husband drinks too much:
out of their gossip, indiscretions
spill like a pint tilted between bar and table.
There are snatches about the price
of leather on each market stall.
The dentist bends over me: beneath
the concentrated muscles of his face
there lies an evident lascivious design
somewhere at the edge of the mouth,
the corner of the eye,
some sexual ventriloquy.
There's a warm stress on her lips,
a whiff of danger circling the excited walls,
something other than the instruments.

2

Outside even Woolworth's is boarded up
and there at the threshold
the holy rollers pump
toward the chilly zenith of heaven
in heavy coats,
with a shared tambourine.

They are rising and falling
with pistons in their knees
on the litter-strewn hill to Calvary.
The dentist cuts across them
with his tree-cutter whine.

3

Under their beards and squat hats
the Bengalis bring their pain,
they have vaults and cavities full of it.
Hands planted on knees,
they're looking down or straight ahead,
to their right the gas fire,
the kind with the bony element
made from patients' teeth.
They have learned to wait
and not to be in a room, like everyone.

4

One of those ten-year-olds
who lead their families
by a thread
like a sheikh in a strange land

enters, with a very old woman,
all dry brown ridges
and sunken mouth and gulleys,
frail bones trapped in white muslin,
ready to fly.

She won't stop her trembling, the dentist
makes moulds of her in soft clay,
sends mosquitoes
and is sorry for the pain.

CONTACT

She came up to him at closing time
among the hulks of breath outside the Cock,
hugging herself, too late
for the preliminary swift half .
well understood among plenty.
"Where d'youse stay?" she said.

He muttered something polite
and disappointing: he could have reached out
and touched her, but he had somewhere to go.
She thanked him, calling him 'mister'
in a way that jarred him out of indifference.
She turned back to the mouth of the Underground.

Neither of them streetwise or proverbial-sly
she was trying this for the first time
and there was still some diffident fantasy
of spontaneous choice, that evaporated
when she thought of waking
to the colourless surprise of a man's back,

shelter meaning much until you have it
like a complicated dream of hunger:
bald towels hung at the bathroom door
like a pair of admonitory crows.
He could hear the rain in the sodden hills
around her shoulders, see the hidden scars

flower to open the contours of irony on her lips,
curling hard among the country syllables.
Like hunks of white bread drifting in pale ale

there were manly expectations in the air:
the best lacked all conviction,
and she knew where to find the rougher trade.

Asleep in their separate lives,
there was an inky silence over the water
but just below, small crustaceans
were busy with secrets and pincers,

using their shells to build settlements,
timescales, lessons and islands
eating all the while in minuscule detail.

Bees came and went on the sea
and they both swam in the whisper,
which in her dream became her father's shout.

STRAWS IN THE WIND

1

His desire for no answer
became a stone at his feet,
became flies and a clock,
a cancer
rising like a fellrunner.

2

Then his name on a list of names:
large-framed village idiots
with shambling cries of welcome
loomed out of the past,
chalk giants with murderous smiles –
one with bulging eyes
and teeth gritted to grin
posing, a cleaver across his crotch.
Their certainties hit him with the boom of foghorns
and populated his wakings.

3

His wife gave him the view he wanted
as an act of faith,
in his sandwich box
the seabirds wheeled
among the blocked traffic like snow.
On his table a small brass secretive lighthouse,
a fulmar gaining height.

4

The small grandeur of the quiet seafront
bent studiously to the mending, changing sea
borrows scale
and a memorable small authority
from the elements.
Seafront houses lean in and back
with the light and the tide;
a memorial leans impossible
heroic breasts out over the sea
where the dead come with their quiet trawlers' lamps
to examine the signs
under a raucous dark clarity of stars.
A winter fly on a book under a lamp
washes its hands slowly.

MATURITY

There was a strange flight in a hammock
through the calls
of red and yellow pleasure-hawks.

I was unable to believe my luck
as strong as a black cauldron
high and simple over the sea.

After the gluttony, clouds
bumped and mingled through the rooms,
I heard the sound of falling rocks
and persistent rain as the house rose
under my uncertain step.

Things have stopped moving.
The sound of games,
clear and youthful, nonsense
among big stones and water.
The house is fully grown,
rooms are projected like arms
like a hunger spread out,
rising through space,
expecting to be met.

THE CHOICE OF FLOWERS

Through the rain's dissolute footsteps
the town's hum is a thing left on a stove,
beginning to cook on its own.
The call of a Boeing
is a fly that passes in the kitchen.
You are a warm light seen from the street,
but I am inside
and still surprised.
Something strange is happening.
I get off a bus in the wrong place
one midsummer dusk
and follow two strangers down a lane
under cascades of wild grass.
I am having an affair with fiction,
the passings, the shadow-life
of time misplaced.
The man didn't think of the woman
until it was too late.
He only thought of her when he was down,
and the thought uplifted him,
and when he saw her again he loved her,
and the years moved him.
And the woman disappeared,
there had been buttonholes and speeches
but no-one there knew
that where she began was much later
when bodies had filled out
and were prone to be comic vehicles
of dignity, courage or regret
and their beauty was a thing
that contained all these.

Someone waves from a life you didn't choose,
from a line of portholes
in a temporary structure,
and you realise the corridor you walk
is a life too.
The trick of familiarity
is a perverse trick,
you are buried in the present,
longing both to rise out of it
and into it.
An illusion of daffodils in the winter gloom
is an act of will or strangeness
and its light underneath your face
makes you look like a ghost.

CONVERSATIONS WITH EMPTINESS

1

Thinking that a mind needs to be emptied
before it is filled well

perhaps I am thinking of a man
spilled into the sky, or vice versa

or a man sawing shelves in his yard.

2

So emptiness runs

from the sticky hives of friends
who celebrate the narrowness of the exits,

from even the impersonal merriment
of alcohol in their eyes,

its own eyes burning with an urgency too serious
without the excuse of youth:

but from a distance they beacon a hilltop dimly
with an undeniable, wry glint

that's buried so deep it stands alongside time,
smoking calmly, and time doesn't see it, abstractedly

playing games with deepening darkness and light,
a little child amused with a Venetian blind.

Then randomly the eyes of emptiness
try on every size in the place

till they become the hulking sun
that scotches intimacies, crumpled thinly

at the roadside, and collapses planets
till surrounding darkness lends proportion to its flame.

3

Emptiness celebrates
the solid inner poise
that rushes out towards it
like the evacuation of a city,
but not just yet,
the shared illusion of mass,

a vibrance of accidental solar gases
coming and going around it,
a half-chance brimming of lifeblood

easily missed if you go for the still centre
with a single-minded faith
of stone in matter, at chapel on soft knees.

The stillness is a stone in one light
safe in its sealed senses,

in another its lengthening shadow,
the massive-shouldered bull
careers down a hillside
to obliterate a small boy
who absently trims a twig:

a stone in itself always perfect in poise

at the same time a magnetic stormlight horizon
a clarity
chased by darkness across the world
chased by clarity.

THE CHIMING AT TRWYN DU

Brilliant as oiled plumage in hollows of sand
at first, the cars' paint
fades in the salt breeze
while their humans peel off into solitude.
The crest of the waves' surge is unbroken,
and the running of the silence is crowned
by the bell off Trwyn Du.
God's cry contracts to a hum
that fades in the current,
there, and there, he cannot
leave it alone, the loud
irregular call of a secretive bird.
There is no passage landward:
we watch, blessed, from the rocks
in the company of the deep-wrinkled mountains.

DECISION

I stood behind a white gate in a still orchard.
Through it, flies milled
and wheeled in the angle of sun
beneath a clasp of sycamores.
Higher, the wind caught saplings
and pulled them and turned every specific leaf
through the light.
In stillness, I watched its purpose
in many fingers pass.

Beads of dew were hung at my feet
in quick movements between
suspicions of movement.
From stillness, the slow gate
opened to the wind's purpose.

The protracted rasp of its hinge.

FOR THE IRISH SEA

The sea is increasingly
a desperate metaphor:
the slimy creatures of the spirit
leave the shells of their body
recklessly in the sand;
when other people are beyond us
we retreat to the sea's
invulnerable dells.
Through swirling banks of weed
at their stations, tangle, dulse
and furbelows, through toothed wrack,
knotted wrack, channelled and spiral,
comes the radioactive word
released by the Secretary
for the Environment.
It churns the careless plankton
slowly with a dispassionate tail.
It is an experiment in barbarism,
a progress crowned.
Its fuel is knowledge
we cannot assimilate.
It has an origin to spoil.

OPTIMISM

Making and unmaking
in their hungry galleries of lacework,
the graceful chains of plankton surge
and dine on carbon-dioxide.

Lady Stanley's hundred-year-old
folly's now an observation tower
and it bristles with technology and pride.
Families queue on the stairs
to pour the special milk of their enjoyment
through a closed circuit camera,
the kind they use in supermarkets,
trained on observant lines of guillemots
that tip down from their shelves
to the sea's churning,
soldiers of optimism
where the surf breaks
among the hungry wilderness of cliffs.
The tower's been licked rough
with white weatherproof
after decades of neglect,
and now it stands out in the radial pulse
of the lighthouse below;
and as the beam sweeps off
and darkness deepens on the sea-pink
in the retina, the turret's white face brushes
with a passing glance of trawlers
that move out there
and are gone among the flashes
of white horse and gannet.
I struggle to persuade myself

that dereliction is made new,
having been once convinced merely
of the folly of its begetter.
There are photographs
of my babyhood in this place,
and the relatives numerous enough
to be visible to the seals
hooting and booming to each other
under the cliffs.
Columns of sunlight move
busy about plankton:
they are gardeners
that thin and rake with ultra-violet.
Look where we will,
the reflection off the rising sea
is volatile.

REFUGEES

A man from Bethnal Green, that
pounded village, said I wrote
of London like some country mouse.
He laid claim, drily, to the voice
out of the dust along the sills
of his delapidated block,
riding as surely as a dibbuk in a trough
behind the combing waves heaved
by his grandparents
like coal across the Baltic
where a pogrom or a near thing
harried them west to land him
lucky with impenetrable coolness
by a steam of notes rising
amplified between paving slabs,
the reassuring shudder
of a subterranean club.

We build our version of arrival
out of grandparents or giant figures
to make and explain us:

his were riding the wave of progress
towards away,
        all effort and belief
in some fleeting credit of heaven
curved beyond them
since refusal often offends –
        all backwash and filthy undertow
as far as they could bring the muddy
complications of their past

            committed as wingless creatures
who believed and understood the principle
of flight, but lacked the mechanics
to stop or return.

As for him, he photographed a riot
quietly, till his camera was taken apart
in a flailing line of police:
he unravelled the film
for the marginal papers,
a memorable geometry of clubs
and perspex shields grown straight
as a stand of windows on the soul.

All are responsible for all
and we mean it in different ways.

At night the streets were filled
with a long migration,
they trailed up the pavement behind us
with their second-hand beginnings
in unruly suitcases
on a sluggish, ankle-deep tide.
Now others are stripped at airports
to their evaporating gratitude,
shoved back on planes
for Sri Lanka, Turkey or Iran –
it takes the duration
of an in-flight movie
to undo the nocturnal escape above the pass
the secret dried meat from a woman in a barn

71

the luck of playing dead behind the dead postman –
this is the ticket to the escape
on rewind to the Kalashnikov butt,
the disposal unit.

On Sunday mornings, in the indifferent
embrace of Stamford Hill, a stooped walk
for bagels symbolised arrival,
with the grandchild's little fingers
preserved in his, the grandfather's hand
preserved in what greater
                           grace and favour –
the Sabbath night
had kept candles alight in the wind.

Later the little apostate cut himself
adrift by the sidelocks, and swam away
mutilated in the darkness
towards his revolution's precious
moment of innocence.
His grandfather saw otherwise:
"He was tied by lines of light
as far as he went, which was not so far:
they were like those lines of headlight
on a postcard he sent us
of the Champs Elysées.
I have smiled at progress now,
and try to make an altar at every step
I have understood."

'Dibbuk' – in Yiddish, a mischievous and possessing spirit.